G000082388

I love Dogs

EDITED BY MARTIN KERR

Helen Exley®

Published in 2015 by Helen Exley® Gift books in Great Britain.
Edited by Martin Kerr
Design, selection and editing © Helen Exley Creative Ltd 2015
Words by Pam Brown, Pamela Dugdale, Helen Exley, Charlotte Gray,
Peter Gray, Stuart & Linda Macfarlane and Helen Thomson © Helen
Exley Creative Ltd 2015.
Photography © Yoneo Morita 2015 Hanadeka™.

ISBN 978-1-84634-980-5

Acknowledgements: The publishers are grateful for permission to
reproduce copyright material. Whilst every reasonable effort has
been made to trace copyright holders, the publishers would be
pleased to hear from any not here acknowledged.

12 11 10 9 8 7 6 5 4 3 2 1

You can follow us on ◼ and ◼

Helen Exley®
16 Chalk Hill, Watford, Herts.
WD19 4BG, UK.
www.helenexley.com

I love Dogs

EDITED BY MARTIN KERR

Helen Exley®

I wag my tail and your blues fade away,
I snuggle close and a frown
turns to a smile, I play catch
and your world turns to laughter.
All I ask in return,
is two meals a day...
and all your love.

STUART & LINDA MACFARLANE

A very small dog
can fill a great gap
in one's life.

PAM BROWN 1928 – 2014

No matter how little money
and how few possessions you own,
having a dog makes you rich.

LOUIS SABIN

He is very imprudent,
a dog is.
...he is going to stick to you,
guard you, give his life for you,
if need be...
You are his pal.

JEROME K. JEROME
1859-1927

All they ask for is the most basic
shelter, food and water,
and in return they give us
unbounding, unflinching affection.

LEO MCKINSTRY,
FROM "DAILY MAIL",
FEBRUARY 18, 2003

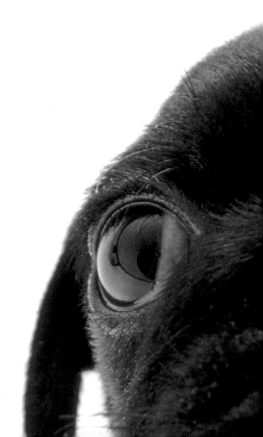

A dog believes you are

who you think you are.

HELEN EXLEY

And when we bury our face
in our hands and wish we had never
been born...
he looks up at you with
his big true eyes, and says with them,
"Well, you've always got me."

JEROME K. JEROME
1859-1927

SIGN ON BULLETIN BOARD

"Puppies for sale:
The only love that money
can buy."

AUTHOR UNKNOWN

...I FELT A SILENT CURRENT
OF LOVE FROM HIM –
STRONG, STEADY AND DEEP...
FOR SOMEONE WHO HAS
NEVER HAD THIS KIND OF
EXPERIENCE, THERE ARE
NO WORDS TO ADEQUATELY
EXPLAIN IT.

SUSAN RACE

The smallest of dogs can fill a room
with love and healing and their
very presence in the home can eliminate
depression and sadness.

BILLY ROBERTS,
FROM "THE HEALING PAW"

Little puppies in pet shops
should have a warning sign
above their cages,
"Don't look into my eyes
or I will kidnap your heart."

STUART & LINDA MACFARLANE

BRAVE LITTLE FELLOW

He was only a little puppy
when he took on the whole world
to defend me.
He was absurdly brave.
And it was there and then
that I determined to return his love
and be all that he expected of me.

HELEN EXLEY

We must choose
the strongest pup,
the cleverest,
the most active.
So why do we choose,
the most helpless, tiny,
tiny dog? All eyes and
rumpled fur.

PAM BROWN 1928 – 2014

Dogs are effervescent, fuzzy marvels of nature.

MARI GAYATRI STEIN

A dog smiles
with its whole face
– ears, eyes, nose, whiskers,
mouth, tongue.

PAM BROWN 1928 – 2014

Every dog deserves
a smile, a word of admiration,
a little reassurance –
especially if he is really ugly
or very sad.

PAM BROWN 1928 – 2014

What jolly chaps they are!
They are much superior to human beings
as companions.
They do not quarrel or argue with you.
They never talk about themselves,
but listen to you
talk about yourself.

JEROME K. JEROME
1859-1927

Dogs have stolen our hearts,
our homes and our wallets,
not necessarily in that order.

AUTHOR UNKNOWN

A dog can talk you into
most things... silently.

PAM BROWN 1928 – 2014

A well-trained dog
will make no attempt to share your lunch.
He will just make you feel so guilty
that you cannot enjoy it.

HELEN EXLEY

The smart dog quickly discovers that,
to get what he wants,
one mournful look is more effective
than a frenzy of barking.

STUART & LINDA MACFARLANE

"Get away, Ugly, you beastly dog!"
he would say. And the dog would be

apparently in an ecstasy of enjoyment
at being called anything at all.

SIR JAMES WALPOLE

There was a clear division
of duties in the house.
Lucky would sit, looking out
of the window, guarding the house
– I would do everything else.

STUART & LINDA MACFARLANE

Here's love.
Disguised as a mop.

PETER GRAY, B. 1928

He is born our friend;
while his eyes are still closed,
already he believes in us:
even before his birth,
he has given himself to man.

COUNT MAURICE MAETERLINCK
1862-1949

I, who had had my heart full for hours,

took advantage of an early moment

of solitude, to cry bitterly.

Suddenly a little hairy head

thrust itself from behind my pillow

into my face...

drying the tears as they came.

ELIZABETH BARRETT BROWNING
1806-1861

HAPPY is the dog
who has found a kind human –
he will forever have someone
to tickle his tummy.

STUART & LINDA MACFARLANE

An abandoned dog, however small,
is totally contented
just being loved, being wanted,
being your companion.

PAMELA DUGDALE

She has crawled
into the deepest corners
of my heart,
the places that hold
the most love –
and the most pain.

CAROLINE KNAPP

A pup is like
a baby.
It goes on trusting
long after it has
been betrayed.

PAM BROWN 1928 – 2014

Our dogs trust us.
They don't question our intentions.
They make us feel good about ourselves,
and we are better people
because of them.

MARI GAYATRI STEIN

We believe in ourselves because of the trust our puppy has in us.

PAM BROWN 1928-2014

A dog is utterly convinced
that its owner is the wisest, kindest
and most skilful
of any in the world.

PETER GRAY, B.1928

Whoever else thinks you
are of little worth –
to your dog you are the heart
of his universe.

PAM BROWN 1928 – 2014

To your dog,
you are more than just a friend;
you are the leader of the pack,
his protector,
his provider, and
an all-knowing god.

STUART & LINDA MACFARLANE

Our dogs will love and admire
the meanest of us,
and feed our colossal vanity
with their uncritical homage.

AGNES REPPLIER
1855-1950

Without dogs the world would seem a lonely place.

LOYD GROSSMAN, FROM
"THE DOG'S TALE"

A dog has one aim in life

There is nothing like the loyalty and love dogs have for their family. Nothing.

MARK R. LEVIN

He was a very bad boy
yet with a heart as boundless as
a summer sky.

JOHN GROGAN

To bestow his heart.

J. R. ACKERLEY

A dull day, a sad day,
a frustrating day – but everything
seems bright when
a small furry object
hurls into your arms
and tells you how very glad
he is to see you home.

PAM BROWN 1928 – 2014

Dog, n.

A kind of additional or
subsidiary Deity
designed to catch the overflow
and surplus
of the world's worship.

AMBROSE BIERCE 1842-1914

Medical studies have shown that people with regular access to dogs visit the doctor less often, have lower blood pressure levels, and suffer fewer incidents of heart disease and dementia. Pet companionship can even increase daily activities and socializing.

STEVE DUNO

She was joyous and beautiful
and a constant symbol
of happiness.
Although she obviously
emulated us,
sometimes I wonder.
Shouldn't I have emulated her?

BROOKS ATKINSON 1894-1984

No matter how badly
we behave, or how low we feel,
dogs are always there to greet us,
full of loyalty and kindness.

LEO MCKINSTRY,
FROM "DAIL MAIL".
FEBRUARY 18, 2003

It doesn't matter whether
we are royalty or rogues;
our dogs don't care
What we are doesn't matter.
Who we are doesn't matter.
our dogs reward us with their loyalty.

JOYCE STRANGER

While I run my toes over his arched spine, I actually feel my tension easing and my bunched up muscles relaxing. I imagine (as most dog owners do) that he "understands" me, understands what I am saying to him.

SHOBHA DÉ

Dogs are great listeners.
You can rattle on for hours
about all your problems –
they won't interrupt even once
and will never, ever criticise.

STUART & LINDA MACFARLANE

A dog can add years
to an old person's life –
someone to care for,
someone to come home to,
someone to talk to.
A dear friend.

PAM BROWN 1928 – 2014

A dog friend just doesn't care
who you are – fat or old or
not too steady on your pins.
Just as long as you love him.

CHARLOTTE GRAY

Soft big eyes,
gentle and quiet.
She is patient
and loving –
just what
any stressed-out
human needs.

HELEN EXLEY

If friends fail us, if the phone
is silent and the postman passes,
our dog will touch our knee,
and smile, and say
all the more time for us to be together.
Come for a walk.
This is a splendid day.

PAM BROWN 1928 – 2014

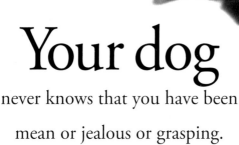

Your dog

never knows that you have been

mean or jealous or grasping.

It encourages you to be

kindly and when you

respond, it loves you.

SIR JAMES WALPOLE

Rarely did he take his beautiful,
kind eyes off me...
and wherever I went there
he would be too,
and wherever I sat he would...
sit beside me –
close, protecting me,
his head on my knee.

ELIZABETH VON ARNIM 1866-1941

To hold a living creature,
to learn its loveliness,
to feel its heart beat in our hands,
to know trust,
is to understand that we are kin.
Is to rejoice in life.
Is to lose all loneliness.

PAM BROWN 1928 – 2014

He is your friend,
your partner, your defender, your dog.
You are his life,
his love,
his leader.
He will be yours
faithful and true,
to the last beat of his heart.

"His name is not Wild Dog
any more, but the First Friend, because
he will be our friend for always
and always and always."

RUDYARD KIPLING 1865-1936

Helen Exley's dogs quotation collection

Helen Exley has specialised in gift books with matching visuals and quotations. Her work has been on finding quotes, mostly of words people would most like to have written themselves, so her books for Mothers and Friends, family and loved ones has sold well over a hundred million copies. Helen has collected dog quotations for dog-lovers over many years. And, in this book, she has matched them to Yoneo Morito's pictures. "I hardly ever write myself, but, just occasionally, I can't resist writing something. I can't own a dog myself, because I travel so often and need to go out to work. It would be cruel. But, I was brought up with four soppy soft Great Danes and I am in love with most dogs I ever meet. So, I broke my normal rule and one or two of my quotations about dogs have somehow popped into this book!" Enjoy! These are the best, most lovable dog quotations and dog pictures we could find.

A note on Yoneo Morita's outstanding photography

Japanese master photographer Yoneo Morita uses fisheye lenses, which distort photographs, for his amazing dog and cat photographs. This kind of lens was originally used scientifically to show maps and astronomical views. In daily life, we use them as front door peephole lenses and for security cameras.

By building on this technique, Yoneo captures and enhances the beautiful, soulful eyes and other endearing features of people's pets. Needless to say, his work began to be in huge demand, and he was inundated by pet-lovers wanting him to catch the most appealing photographs possible of their beloved cats and dogs. Many years later, with a collection then running to thousands of photos of cats, dogs - and indeed ducks and hamsters - his work started to be used all around the world, for gifts like greeting cards, mugs, and calendars.

And then came his gift book collections, created by Helen Exley, where Yoneo Morita's most lovable cat and dog pictures have been matched with quotations. These collections have gone on to sell hundreds of thousands of copies.